What Is Climate?

by Jennifer Boothroyd

Lerner Publications Company · Minneapolis

LERNER

SOURCE™

Expand learning beyond the printed book. Download free, complementary educational resources for this book from our website, www.lerneresource.com.

The images in this book are used with the permission of: © iStockphoto.com/CEFutcher, p. 4; © Ryan McVay/Photodisc/Thinkstock, p. 5; © iStockphoto.com/kali9, p. 6; © Ingrid Prats/Shutterstock.com, p. 7; © Katrina Leigh/Shutterstock.com, p. 8; © Dennis MacDonald/SuperStock, p. 9; © Fineart11/Shutterstock.com, p. 10; © T.W. van Urk/Shutterstock.com, p. 11; © iStockphoto.com/youngvet, p. 12; © CandyBox Images/Shutterstock.com, p. 13; © Fedor Slivanov/Shutterstock.com, p. 14; © Dennis MacDonald/SuperStock, p. 15; © AridOcean/Shutterstock.com, p. 16; © Mayskyphoto/Shutterstock.com, p. 17; © Steven Dahlman/SuperStock, p. 18; © SeanPavonePhoto/Shutterstock.com, p. 19; © Ysbrand Cosijn/Shutterstock.com, p. 20; © romakoma/Shutterstock.com, p. 21.

Front cover: © Karolina Grabara/iStock/Thinkstock

Main body text set in ITC Avant Garde Gothic Std Medium 21/25.
Typeface provided by Adobe Systems.

Lerner Publications Company
A division of Lerner Publishing Group, Inc.
241 First Avenue North
Minneapolis, MN 55401 USA

For reading levels and more information, look up this title at www.lernerbooks.com.

Library of Congress Cataloging-in-Publication Data

The Cataloging-in-Publication Data for *What is Climate?* is on file at the Library of Congress.
ISBN: 978–1–4677–3918–4 (LB)
ISBN: 978–1–4677–4681–6 (EB)

Manufactured in the United States of America
1 – CG – 7/15/14

Table of Contents

Weather and Climate

Weather happens every day.

Some days are rainy.

5

These kids cool off in a pool.

Some days are hot.

Seasons are patterns.

Weather happens in **patterns**.

These cactuses grow in a dry climate.

The weather patterns of a place over many years make up the **climate**.

Studying Climate

Computers are one tool for studying climate.

Scientists study climate.

They measure the
temperature of the air.

They measure how much
rain falls.

They measure how much snow falls.

They measure the **height** of the land.

Snow covers these mountaintops.

It is cooler high in the mountains.

Scientists look for climate changes.

North America's Climate

This is our continent.

Our **continent** has different climates.

Northern Canada has cool summers.

These photos show Minnesota's seasons.

Minnesota has warm summers and snowy winters.

It rarely snows in Georgia.

The Mojave Desert is dry.

It is hot in southern Mexico.

What is the climate like where you live?

Glossary

climate – the weather patterns in an area over time

continent – one of the seven large land areas on Earth

height – the distance from top to bottom

patterns – things that happen in a regular or repeated way

temperature – the measurement of heat or cold

weather – what happens in the outside air

Index